Farm To Table:

50 Recipes For Clean Eating

MouseWorks Publishing is an indie publisher with one simple mission: Make books you want to read!

Follow us and be the first to know about new releases and free promotions!

www.facebook.com/mouseworkspub

http://www.twitter.com/mouseworkspub

Table of Contents

What is Clean Eating?

What is clean eating? It's not rocket science and it's not a diet trend. Eating clean is simply about eating foods that are more natural and simple. The idea is to stay away from foods that are processed and have preservatives.

Consuming only farm fresh vegetables, meats, and whole grains is the purest form of clean eating. However, many people find success changing their lifestyle, becoming healthier, and discovering how truly delicious natural foods can be by using a clean eating rule of thumb at the grocery store or local farmer's market. Using moderation when selecting food choices is a great way to ease into the clean eating movement.

This book provides 50 of the very best recipes for clean eating and focuses on farm fresh ingredients. It's perfect for clean eating novices as well as those who are just looking for more scrumptious farm to table recipes.

Appetizers and Sides

Oven Roasted Asparagus

Preparation time: 5 minutes

Total time: 21 minutes

Yield: 4

Ingredients:

5 tablespoons olive oil

3 garlic cloves

2 tablespoons shallot thinly sliced

Salt and pepper to taste

1 and ½ pound asparagus stemmed

2 lemon wedges

Directions:

1. Preheat oven to 400 degrees F.

2. Combine olive oil, garlic, shallots, salt, pepper, and asparagus.

3. Pour bowl into heavy bottomed glass baking dish and roast for 12-16 minutes, turning half way through.

4. Remove from oven, sprinkle with lemon, and serve.

Fresh Cucumber Salsa

Preparation time: 10 minutes

Total time: 1 hr and 10 minutes

Yield: 12

Ingredients:

2 cucumbers chopped

2 tomatoes chopped

½ cup orange bell pepper chopped

1 yellow onion chopped

1 jalapeno pepper finely chopped

1 garlic clove minced

1 teaspoon parsley chopped

2 tablespoons lime juice

½ teaspoon dill weed

⅛ teaspoon salt

12 ounces package tortilla chips for serving

Directions:

1. In a large salad bowl, combine cucumbers, tomatoes, jalapenos, bell peppers, onion, and garlic.

2. Add dill, parsley, salt and lime juice and toss to coat.

3. Refrigerate at least 1 hour before serving or make the night before and leave in fridge overnight.

4. Serve with tortilla chips.

Cucumber And Peanut Salad

Preparation time: 10 minutes

Total time: 15 minutes

Yield: 2

Ingredients:

1 large cucumber cubed

1 tablespoon butter

¼ teaspoon kosher salt

½ teaspoon dried red pepper flakes

½ teaspoon cumin

1 lemon cut into wedges

3 tablespoons peanuts chopped

1 teaspoon agave nectar

1 teaspoon cilantro finely chopped

Directions:

1. In a strainer, combine cucumber and salt; set aside for 10 minutes to release water

2. Pat dry and transfer to a salad bowl.

3. Heat a saucepan to medium and melt butter.

4. Add nectar, red pepper flakes and cumin and stir well.

5. Remove from heat, then add peanuts and stir.

6. Pour mixture over cucumbers and stir until well

combined.

7. Sprinkle cilantro on top and serve with lemon wedges

Mexican Street Corn

Preparation time: 5 minutes

Total time: 35 minutes

Yield: 6

Ingredients:

6 ears of corn

6 tablespoons butter

½ cup mayonnaise or Mexican crema

½ cup queso fresco

½ cup crumbled feta

1 teaspoon chili powder

½ teaspoon cayenne

2 garlic cloves minced

1 lime cut into wedges

Salt and pepper to taste

Directions:

1. Preheat grill to high heat or oven to 400 degrees F.

2. Peel back corn husks and remove silk. Coat each ear with 1 tablespoon butter, salt and pepper. Cover in husks and wrap in aluminum foil.

3. Place directly onto grill or oven racks and cook for 30 minutes turning every 10 minutes.

4. Meanwhile, combine cheeses, chili powder,

cayenne and garlic in small bowl.

5. Remove corn from oven and allow to cool until safe to touch.

6. Peel husks down and spread mayonnaise/crema evenly on corn. Then sprinkle seasoning mixture until well coated.

7. Serve with lime wedges.

Whole Baked Beets

Preparation time: 10 minutes

Total time: 2 hours

Yield: 4

Ingredients:

¾ cup chopped walnuts

1 tablespoon butter

4 beets washed and trimmed

2 cups plain yogurt

1 green chili pepper chopped

Salt and pepper to taste

Directions:

1. Preheat oven to 375 degrees F.

2. Heat small skillet to medium low, add walnuts and stir constantly until walnuts are golden, then set aside to cool.

3. Coat aluminum foil with butter, pierce beets with fork, wrap in foil, and bake in the oven for 1 hour.

4. Remove beets from the oven and let cool.

5. Meanwhile, combine yogurt, green chili pepper and walnuts in a bowl.

6. Season with salt and pepper and leave aside for 30 minutes.

7. Unwrap beets, peel them, cut into quarters most of the way. Leave them intact at the bottom.

8. Spoon in yogurt mixture and serve.

Grilled Bell Peppers And Goat Cheese

Preparation time: 7 minutes

Total time: 15 minutes

Yield: 6

Ingredients:

2 large green bell peppers

2 tablespoons olive oil

1 garlic clove minced

Salt and pepper to taste

1 lemon cut into wedges

½ cup goat cheese

Directions:

1. Cut bell peppers lengthwise into 6 wedges, seed and core them and place in mixing bowl.

2. Add garlic and oil. Toss to coat and set aside.

3. Preheat grill to high and cook bell peppers for about 3-5 minutes until skin is charred.

4. Remove peppers and set aside.

5. In a bowl, combine goat cheese, 2 wedges of lemon, salt and pepper.

6. Stuff peppers with goat cheese, place back on grill and cook for 3 more minutes.

7. Serve with additional lemon wedges.

Farmer's Bruschetta

Preparation time: 5 minutes

Total time: 15 minutes

Yield: 6

Ingredients:

3 vine ripened tomatoes diced

2 tablespoons basil chopped

1 tablespoon balsamic vinegar

½ cup parmesan grated

2 cloves garlic minced

1 tablespoon olive oil

1 whole wheat baguette

Directions:

1. Preheat oven to 350 degrees F.

2. Slice baguette and place on baking sheet. Sprinkle with garlic and drizzle with olive oil. Then bake for about 5 minutes or until crispy and golden.

3. Meanwhile, combine tomatoes, basil, and balsamic vinegar.

4. Spoon tomatoes on baguette slices, sprinkle parmesan and serve.

Chickpea Feta Salad

Preparation time: 5 minutes

Total time: 1 hour and 5 minutes

Yield: 6

Ingredients:

1 ½ cups chickpeas

1 cup cherry tomatoes

6 oz feta cheese crumbles

1 tablespoon oregano

2 tablespoons olive oil

Butter lettuce

Salt and pepper to taste

Directions:

1. In a blender, combine chickpeas, tomatoes, feta, and olive oil. Pulse to blend.

2. Add oregano, salt and pepper and mix well. Transfer to storage container and refrigerate at least 1 hour or overnight.

3. Transfer to a serving bowl and serve in butter lettuce leaves.

Summer Tomato Salad

Preparation time: 5 minutes

Total time: 15 minutes

Yield: 6

Ingredients:

1 cup fresh snow peas

2 pounds heirloom tomatoes sliced

3 basil leaves minced

6 ounces feta cheese crumbled

Salt and pepper to taste

For the basil dressing:

⅓ cup coconut oil

⅓ cup basil minced

1 tablespoon mustard

1 lemon

Salt to taste

½ teaspoon crushed red pepper

Directions:

1. Zest lemon and slice into wedges.

2. Add oil, minced basil, mustard, lemon zest, red pepper, juice from 1 lemon wedge and salt in blender and mix well.

3. Meanwhile, heat a saucepan to medium and add

about an inch of water. Cook peas for 5 minutes, drain, blanch in ice water 5 minutes, remove and pat dry.

4. Combine peas and dressing in a mixing bowl and toss.

5. Place tomatoes on serving plates, add peas with dressing, basil, cheese, salt and pepper.

6. Serve with lemon wedges.

Okra And Sweet Potato Hash

Preparation time: 5 minutes

Total time: 20 minutes

Yield: 6

Ingredients:

⅓ cup coconut oil

1 yellow onion minced

2 garlic cloves minced

2 teaspoons grated ginger

½ pound sweet potatoes diced

½ teaspoon red pepper flakes

Salt to taste

1 and ½ pound fresh okra thinly sliced

2 teaspoons cumin

1 teaspoon turmeric

2 teaspoons coriander

1 tablespoon mustard powder

2 tablespoons sesame seeds toasted

Directions:

1. Heat large heavy bottomed skillet to medium high. Add oil and cook onions until translucent (about 3 minutes.)

2. Add garlic and ginger and cook for 1 more minute.

3. Add potatoes, red pepper flakes, salt, cover skillet and cook for 5-6 minutes stirring occasionally.

4. Uncover, add okra, cumin, coriander, mustard powder, and turmeric, stir and cook for 10 more minutes.

5. Remove from heat and transfer to serving plates. Sprinkle with sesame seeds and serve.

Roasted Indian Okra

Preparation time: 5 minutes

Total time: 15 minutes

Yield: 6

Ingredients:

Zest from 1 lime

1 lime cut in 8 wedges

2 pounds fresh okra

1 tablespoon cumin

½ teaspoon coriander

2 garlic cloves chopped

2 tablespoons extra virgin olive oil

Salt and pepper to taste

¼ cup cilantro chopped

Directions:

1. In a bowl, mix okra with lime zest, olive oil, garlic, cumin, coriander, salt and pepper.

2. Heat oven to 350 degrees F

3. Place okra on baking sheet and cook for 10 minutes, turning them half way through.

4. Transfer to a platter, sprinkle cilantro on top and serve with lime wedges.

Squash with Tomatillo Salsa

Preparation time: 5 minutes

Total time: 20 minutes

Yield: 6

Ingredients:

5 medium assorted squash cut into ¼ inch slices

½ teaspoon kosher salt

3 tablespoons olive oil

1 cup pepitas, shelled, unsalted and toasted

¼ cup feta cheese

For the salsa:

7 tomatillos

Salt to taste

½ white onion chopped

2 tablespoons cilantro minced

2 tablespoons lime juice

Directions:

1. Heat skillet to medium and add tomatillos, onion and salt to taste.

2. Cook for 3 minutes, drain and transfer to blender or use a hand blender.

3. Add lime juice and cilantro and blend well.

4. Meanwhile, preheat oven to 350 degrees F, place

squash on baking sheet, drizzle with olive oil and bake 10-12 minutes.

5. Transfer squash to a serving platter, add pepitas, feta cheese and drizzle with tomatillo salsa.

Zucchini Soup

Preparation time: 10 minutes

Total time: 40 minutes

Yield: 6

Ingredients:

½ cup fennel bulb diced

½ cup sweet onion diced

1 tablespoon extra virgin olive oil

3 garlic cloves minced

5 cups zucchini diced

1 cup water

2 cups vegetable stock

Salt to taste

2 teaspoons white wine vinegar

Zest and juice from 1 lemon

Directions:

1. Heat a Dutch oven to medium high and add oil. Cook onion and fennel for 5 minutes.

2. Add zucchini and garlic. Cook for 3 more minutes.

3. Add water, stock, stir, bring to a simmer and cook for 25 minutes.

4. Remove from heat, transfer to blender (or use hand blender) and blend until smooth and creamy.

5. Add salt, vinegar, lemon juice and zest and blend again.

6. Pour in serving bowls. Maybe served hot or refrigerate 2 hours and serve cold.

Roasted Eggplant With Miso Glaze

Preparation time: 10 minutes

Total time: 15 minutes

Yield: 6

Ingredients:

⅓ cup plain yogurt

2 tablespoons white miso

2 eggplants sliced lengthwise

¼ cup cilantro rough chopped

¼ cup extra virgin olive oil

¼ teaspoon black pepper

Salt to taste

1 small lime

Directions:

1. Preheat oven to 350 degrees F.

2. In a mixing bowl, combine yogurt, miso, lime juice and black pepper. Then set aside.

3. Brush each eggplant slice with olive oil and season with salt and pepper.

4. Place eggplant on baking sheet and cook for 10 minutes, flipping half way through.

5. Transfer to a serving platter, drizzle with miso glaze and top with cilantro.

Baba Ganoush

Preparation time: 30 minutes

Total time: 1 hour

Yield: 6

Ingredients:

2 eggplants

¼ cup tahini

¼ cup lemon juice

4 garlic cloves minced

½ teaspoon salt

¼ teaspoon cumin

2 tablespoons parsley roughly chopped

1 ½ tablespoon extra virgin olive oil

Directions:

1. Preheat broiler. Place eggplants on a baking sheet, prick them with a fork, broil them at a high temperature for 2 minutes on each side.

2. Remove from broiler, and turn oven down to 375 degrees F. Roast for 20 minutes.

3. Remove from oven and allow to cool for 8 minutes.

4. Meanwhile, combine tahini, garlic, lemon juice, salt and cumin in a small mixing bowl.

5. Cut eggplants in half, scrape out flesh and place in

a mixing bowl.

6. Combine eggplant flesh with tahini and mix until well combined.

7. Allow to cool at room temperature, add parsley and drizzle olive oil.

Entrees

Stuffed Mushroom

Preparation time: 5 minutes

Total time: 50 minutes

Yield: 6

Ingredients:

6 large portabella mushrooms

1 pound ground sausage

1 tablespoon fennel

1 teaspoon red pepper flakes

½ tablespoon onion powder

2 cloves garlic minced

1 cup parmesan cheese grated

8 oz cream cheese room temperature

Salt and pepper to taste

Directions:

1. Preheat oven to 375 degrees F.

2. Wash and pat dry mushrooms. Remove stalks and chop. Set aside.

3. Heat a medium sized skillet to medium high and cook sausage and mushroom stalks 5-6 minutes. Add

salt and pepper as needed.

4. Meanwhile use a hand mixer to combine cream cheese, parmesan, garlic, onion powder, red pepper flakes, and fennel.

5. Strain grease from sausage and pour sausage into cream cheese mixture.

6. Use hand mixer to blend until well combined.

7. Spoon mixture generously on mushroom tops and place on ungreased baking sheet

8. Cook about 40 minutes or until mushrooms are tender.

9. Remove from oven and serve.

Cajun Stuffed Peppers

Preparation time: 30 minutes

Total time: 50 minutes

Yield: 6

Ingredients:

6 large green bell peppers

1 yellow onion minced

3 tablespoons olive oil

1 tablespoon creole seasoning

2 garlic cloves minced

¾ teaspoon oregano

¼ teaspoon black pepper

1 tablespoon of salt

2 links andouille sausage chopped

2 cups chicken broth

1 cup brown rice uncooked

8 ounces tomato sauce

Directions:

1. Grease a baking dish and set aside. Preheat oven to 325 degrees F.

2. Bring a large pot of salted water to a boil

3. Remove tops from peppers, cook them for 3 minutes, drain and transfer to a bowl of ice water for 3

minutes. Then pat dry and set aside.

4. Heat large heavy bottomed skillet to medium. Add oil and onions. Cook for 3 minutes.

5. Add garlic, oregano, creole seasoning and black pepper and stir.

6. Add sausage and cook for 5 minutes.

7. Add rice and cook for 1 minute.

8. Add tomato sauce and broth, stir and simmer until it thickens for 15 minutes.

9. Fill peppers with this mix, place in greased baking dish and bake in oven for 15 minutes.

10. Remove from oven and serve.

Not Your Grandma's Chicken Salad Wrap

Preparation time: 5 minutes

Total time: 10 minutes

Yield: 6

Ingredients:

3 tablespoons olive oil

2 and ½ teaspoons agave nectar

3 tablespoons white wine vinegar

Salt and pepper to taste

3 cups already cooked chicken shredded

1 ½ cups white mushrooms sliced

2 pounds heirloom tomatoes cut in small wedges

½ cup red onion thinly sliced

2 tablespoons basil roughly chopped

4 green onions sliced

2 tablespoons parsley roughly chopped

1 tablespoon thyme

12 whole wheat tortillas

Directions:

1. In a mixing bowl, combine olive oil, nectar, vinegar, basil, parsley, thyme, red onions, green onions, salt, pepper and stir well.

2. Gently fold in tomatoes and chicken.

3. Wrap in whole wheat tortillas and serve.

Roasted Pork Shoulder

Preparation time: 30 minutes

Total time: 8 hours

Yield: 6

Ingredients:

6 cloves garlic minced

6 pound pork shoulder or butt

2 tablespoons salt

1 tablespoon black pepper

1 tablespoon coffee grounds

1 tablespoon cumin

½ tablespoon smoked paprika

½ tablespoon mustard powder

½ tablespoon coriander

2 tablespoons onion powder

3 tablespoons brown sugar

Directions:

1. In a small mixing bowl, combine salt, pepper, coffee grounds, cumin, paprika, mustard powder, coriander, onion powder, and brown sugar.

2. Pat pork shoulder dry and coat in seasonings.

3. Place in crock pot on low heat for 8 hours.

4. Serve with your favorite side and whole wheat rolls.

Crusted Rosemary Veal Chops

Preparation time: 10 minutes

Total time: 20 minutes

Yield: 4

Ingredients:

Some whole wheat flour for dredging

3 eggs

1 ½ tablespoons almond milk

4 veal rib chops

5 tablespoons extra virgin olive oil

4 sprigs fresh rosemary

2 cloves garlic minced

Salt and pepper to taste

Directions:

1. Preheat oven to 350 degrees F.

2. Place whole wheat flour in a shallow bowl.

3. In a mixing bowl, whisk eggs, milk, salt and pepper.

4. Season veal chops with garlic, rosemary, salt and pepper and dredge them in flour.

5. Then dip in egg mix and dredge in flour again.

6. Heat a large skillet to medium heat and add olive oil. Add veal chops, cook for 2 minutes, flip them and cook for another 3 minutes until brown.

7. Place chops on baking sheet and bake 15 minutes.

8. Remove from oven and serve.

Easy Spaghetti

Preparation time: 5 minutes

Total time: 25 minutes

Yield: 6

Ingredients:

1 pound whole wheat spaghetti

1 ½ pounds ground beef

28 oz crushed tomatoes

1 tablespoon olive oil

1 yellow onion minced

1 carrot finely chopped

1 celery stick finely chopped

1 green bell pepper finely chopped

1 tablespoon butter

3 cloves garlic minced

½ teaspoon black pepper

1 tablespoon Italian seasoning

3 tablespoons parsley roughly chopped

salt to taste

Parmesan to taste

Directions:

1. Bring a large pot of water to a boil. Cook pasta

according to package directions. Drain and set aside.

2. Meanwhile, heat a large skillet over medium heat. Add oil, onion, carrot, celery, and bell pepper. Saute until onion begins to brown, about 5-7 minutes.

3. Stir in garlic and Italian seasoning; cook about 30 seconds. Add ground beef and cook 5 minutes or until brown.

4. Turn to high heat and stir in tomatoes. Cook 5 minutes. Stir in parsley, salt and pepper. Remove from heat and stir in butter.

5. Serve the sauce over the pasta, sprinkled with parmesan.

Crusted Roast Beef

Preparation time: 10 minutes

Total time: 2 hours and 30 minutes

Yield: 8

Ingredients:

6 pounds sirloin roast

½ cup prepared horseradish mix

2 tablespoons salt

2 tablespoons mustard powder

2 tablespoons parsley roughly chopped

1 tablespoon ground black pepper

1 tablespoon maple syrup

1 tablespoon sherry vinegar

Directions:

1. Preheat oven to 375 degrees F.

2. In a mixing bowl, combine horseradish, salt, mustard powder, pepper, parsley, syrup and vinegar.

3. Rub over meat to coat, place in a roasting pan, and bake for 2 hours.

4. Remove from oven, let cool 20 minutes. Then slice and serve.

Sweet and Sassy Slow Cooker Pork Chops

Preparation time: 15 minutes

Total time: 7 hours and 15 minutes

Yield: 6

Ingredients:

6 bone-in pork chops

1 teaspoon salt

1 teaspoon black pepper

2 tablespoons onion powder

3 garlic cloves minced

¼ cup cayenne

¼ cup brown sugar

¼ cup olive oil

Directions:

1. In a mixing bowl, combine salt, pepper, onion powder, garlic, cayenne, and brown sugar.

2. Brush pork chops with olive oil and coat with seasoning rub.

3. Place in crock pot and cook on high 4 hours or low 7- 8 hours.

4. Remove chops from crock pot and serve.

Roast Lemon Herb Chicken

Preparation time: 15 minutes

Total time: 2 hours and 15 minutes

Yield: 4

Ingredients:

1 whole chicken

1 red onion roughly chopped

4 lemons halved and juiced

½ teaspoon salt

½ teaspoon black pepper

8 garlic cloves minced

3 sprigs rosemary

1 bay leaf

3 sprigs thyme

⅓ cup olive oil

Directions:

1. Put chicken in large zip top bag.

2. Add remaining ingredients.

3. Close bag, shake well and keep in the refrigerator for 1 hour.

4. Preheat oven to 425 degrees F.

5. Remove chicken from fridge and place in glass baking dish. Pour remaining marinade in dish and

bake for 45 minutes.

6. Remove oven, leave to cool down for 15 minutes, then serve.

Habanero Plum Chicken Breast

Preparation time: 20 minutes

Total time: 40 minutes

Yield: 2

Ingredients:

1 cup uncooked quinoa

1 and ½ vegetable broth

¾ pound plums chopped

½ red onion minced

1 habanero pepper finely chopped

Salt and pepper to taste

1 teaspoon honey

1 pound boneless skinless chicken breasts

3 sprigs rosemary

2 teaspoons coconut oil

Directions:

1. Add broth to a saucepan, heat to medium temperature, add quinoa, bring to a boil, cook for 20 minutes, remove from stove, cool down, fluff with a fork and set aside.

2. Meanwhile, combine onion, pepper, plums, and honey in mixing bowl and set aside.

3. Season chicken with salt, pepper and rosemary.

4. Heat skillet to medium high. Add oil and chicken. Cook 1 minute on each side.

5. Reduce temperature to medium and cook for 5 minutes on each side.

6. Transfer chicken on serving plates and serve with plum salsa.

Maple Apple Stuffed Chicken

Preparation time: 20 minutes

Total time: 30 minutes

Yield: 4

Ingredients:

4 chicken breasts

1 apple peeled and thinly sliced

1 egg

1 tablespoon mustard

1 tablespoon maple syrup

⅔ cup whole wheat flour

⅔ cup pecans chopped

Salt and pepper to taste

3 tablespoons coconut oil

Directions:

1. In a mixing bowl, combine flour, salt, pepper and pecans.

2. In another dish, mix egg with maple syrup and mustard.

3. Cut pockets in each chicken breast and fill them with apple slices.

4. Dip each piece in flour, egg mixture, and flour again.

5. Heat skillet to medium and add oil and chicken. Cook for 3 minutes on each side. Reduce heat and cook an additional 3-4 minutes until juices run clear.

6. Remove chicken and serve.

Cheeseburger Wraps

Preparation time: 10 minutes

Total time: 30 minutes

Yield: 4

Ingredients:

1 pound ground beef

2 garlic cloves chopped

¼ teaspoon ground oregano

Salt and pepper to taste

8 ounces cheddar cheese shredded

1 white onion sliced

1 tomato sliced

1 tablespoon olive oil

½ head romaine lettuce

4 whole wheat tortillas

Directions:

1. Heat skillet with the oil to medium high and caramelize the onion for 15 minutes stirring all the time.

2. Heat another skillet to medium high and brown the beef for 5-7 minutes.

3. Add salt, pepper, oregano and garlic, stir well and remove from heat.

4. Place each tortilla wrap on a working surface, add beef, cheese, caramelized onions, tomatoes, lettuce, wrap tortillas and serve.

Herb Roasted Turkey

Preparation time: 30 minutes

Total time: 4 hours

Yield: 10

Ingredients:

1 fresh whole turkey

Zest and juice from 1 lemon

½ cup butter

1 tablespoon coconut oil

½ shallot chopped

8 sage leaves

1 tablespoon rosemary

2 tablespoon thyme leaves

1 garlic clove chopped

1 yellow onion

2 carrots

2 celery stalks

1 cup dry white wine

1 cup chicken stock

¼ cup whole wheat flour

Directions:

1. Combine lemon zest and juice with butter, shallot,

sage, thyme, rosemary and garlic. Place in refrigerator to chill.

2. Wash turkey, drain cavity well, remove neck and giblets, pat dry it with paper towels, lift skin from turkey breast without detaching it, rub it with 3 tablespoons of the herb butter under the skin and secure with toothpicks.

3. Preheat oven to 425 degrees F.

4. Season the cavity and the whole turkey with salt and pepper to the taste and place in a glass baking dish.

5. Also arrange onion, carrots and celery in the same dish.

6. Tie ends of turkey legs together, rub the turkey with the rest of herb butter, add wine and stock to the pan, and bake for 30 minutes.

7. Reduce heat to 325 degrees F and bake for 2 hours and 30 minutes.

8. Remove turkey from the oven, leave aside for 20 minutes, transfer to a platter, pour veggie drippings through a strainer and reserve 2 and ½ cups of drippings.

9. Heat skillet to medium, add oil and flour, stir well and cook for 2 minutes.

10. Add reserved pan drippings, bring to a boil, reduce the temperature and cook for 6 minutes stirring occasionally.

11. Cut turkey and serve with the gravy.

Farmer's Vegetable Soup

Preparation time: 15 minutes

Total time: 45 minutes

Yield: 6

Ingredients:

5 cups vegetable stock

1 cup tomato puree

14 oz diced tomatoes

1 cup corn

1 cup peas

1 cup carrots sliced

3 celery stalks chopped

1 red bell pepper sliced

1 green bell pepper

1 zucchini sliced

1 tablespoon garlic salt

1 tablespoon olive oil

1 yellow onion minced

¾ cup water

Directions:

1. Heat a large pot to medium high and add add olive oil and onions. Cook about 2 minutes.

2. Then add vegetable stock, tomato puree, diced tomatoes, olive oil and water. Stir to combine and bring to a simmer.

3. Add corn, peas, carrots, celery, peppers and zucchini. Stir in garlic salt.

4. Continue to simmer, stirring occasionally, for 25 minutes.

5. Remove from heat and serve in soup bowls.

Delicious Corn Soup

Preparation time: 10 minutes

Total time: 30 minutes

Yield: 4

Ingredients:

15 ears of corn, removed from cob

2 carrots chopped

2 yellow onions minced

2 garlic cloves minced

3 tablespoons olive oil

6 green onions

10 springs thyme

5 quarts vegetable stock

Salt and pepper to taste

Directions:

1. Heat up a pot with the oil at a medium temperature and cook onion and carrots until onion becomes translucent (about 3 minutes.)

2. Add garlic, stir and cook for 1 more minute.

3. Add corn kernels and cook for 10 minutes stirring constantly.

4. Add stock and thyme, bring to a boil and simmer for 10 minutes.

5. Add salt and pepper and stir

6. Remove from heat and discard thyme.

7. Pour into blender or use a hand blender and puree until smooth

8. Pour through a strainer and transfer to soup bowls.

9. Sprinkle with green onions and serve hot.

Lemon Dill Salmon

Preparation time: 5 minutes

Total time: 15 minutes

Yield: 4

Ingredients:

4 Salmon fillets

1 tablespoon dill

Zest and juice from 1 lemon

1 tablespoon olive oil

Salt and pepper to taste

Directions:

1. Preheat cast iron skillet to high heat.

2. Wash and pat dry fish. Then season with dill, lemon zest, salt and pepper. Brush with olive oil and add to skillet skin side down.

3. Immediately turn heat down to medium and cook 3 minutes. Squeeze 1 lemon wedge on fish and flip. Cook an additional 5 minutes.

4. Serve with lemon wedges.

Chili Lime Talapia

Preparation time: 5 minutes

Total time: 10 minutes

Yield: 4

Ingredients:

4 Talapia fillets

2 tablespoons chili powder

Zest and juice from 1 lime

1 tablespoon olive oil

Salt and pepper to taste

Directions:

1. Preheat cast iron skillet to high heat.

2. Wash and pat dry fish. Then season with chili powder, lime zest, salt and pepper. Brush with olive oil and add to skillet.

3. Cook about 3 minutes on each side until inside is white and glistens.

4. Serve with lime wedges.

Breakfast

Breakfast Casserole

Preparation time: 10 minutes

Total time: 1 hour 30 minutes

Yield: 4

Ingredients:

6 large eggs

⅓ cup coconut milk

1 large red bell pepper, chopped

1 cup sweet potatoes grated

1 pound ground sausage

1 tablespoon coconut oil

1 tablespoon garlic powder

1 tablespoon onion powder

1 tablespoon basil

1 teaspoon black pepper

Salt to taste

Directions:

1. Preheat oven to 350 F.

1. Heat a skillet to medium and add oil and sausage. Cook until browned. Drain.

2. Meanwhile, whisk eggs, milk, basil, garlic powder,

onion powder and pepper in a large mixing bowl.

3. Fold in bell pepper, sweet potatoes, and cooked sausage.

4. Pour into glass baking dish and bake 50-60 minutes.

5. Allow to cool 7 minutes. Then serve.

Mushroom and Tomato Breakfast Hash

Preparation time: 10 minutes

Total time: 20 minutes

Yield: 4

Ingredients:

1 cup sliced portabella mushrooms

½ cup extra virgin olive oil

½ pound cherry tomatoes chopped

¼ cup basil chopped

4 eggs poached

Salt and pepper to taste

Directions:

1. Preheat non-stick skillet to medium and add mushrooms. Saute 8-10 minutes.

2. Add oil and tomatoes and cook for 8 minutes, stirring constantly.

3. Add basil, salt and pepper, stir, cook for 1 minutes.

4. Transfer to serving plates and top with poached eggs.

Almond Cereal

Preparation time: 5 minutes

Total time: 35 minutes

Yield: 4

Ingredients:

2 cups whole almonds

⅓ cup coconut oil

4 pitted dates

1 cup pumpkin seeds

1 tablespoon brown sugar

1 tablespoon vanilla extract

2 teaspoons cinnamon

½ teaspoon kosher salt

¾ cup coconut flakes

¾ cup wheat bran

Directions:

1. Preheat oven to 300 degrees F.

2. Put half the almonds and pumpkin seeds, coconut oil, and dates in a food processor. Pulse until ground.

3. Add the remaining pecans and pumpkin seeds and pulse until roughly chopped.

4. Transfer to a mixing bowl and add the bran, vanilla, brown sugar, cinnamon and salt. Stir and spread on a

baking sheet.

5. Bake for about 25-30 minutes, until golden brown. Remove, allow to cool, and stir in the coconut flakes.

6. Store in an airtight container until ready to serve.

Walnut and Cranberry Oatmeal

Preparation time: 5 minutes

Total time: 20 minutes

Yield: 4

Ingredients:

2 cups almond milk

1 cup water

¼ teaspoon kosher salt

1 cup steel cut oats

1 tablespoon honey

1 teaspoon vanilla extract

½ cup walnuts chopped

½ teaspoon cinnamon

¼ teaspoon nutmeg

¼ cup dried cranberries

Directions:

1. In a medium saucepan, combine almond milk, water and salt and bring to a boil.

2. Add oats, cover and reduce heat to a simmer. Cook 10- 20 minutes to desired consistency.

3. Remove from heat and stir in walnuts, vanilla extract, cinnamon, nutmeg and honey.

4. Top with cranberries and serve.

Bacon Spinach Frittata

Preparation time: 10 minutes

Total time: 30 minutes

Yield: 4

Ingredients:

8 large eggs

1 tablespoon extra virgin olive oil

6 strips bacon

5 cups spinach chopped

Salt and black pepper to taste

Directions:

1. Preheat oven to 350F.

2. In a mixing bowl, whisk the eggs with the oil and set aside.

3. Add bacon to a cold iron skillet and heat to medium. Cook until crispy. Remove bacon and set on paper towel. Leave bacon fat in skillet.

4. Add the spinach to the skillet and cook until just wilted.

5. Meanwhile, add crumble bacon and add to egg mixture. Then pour mixture in skillet and season with salt and pepper.

6. Transfer to oven and bake for 20 minutes, until eggs are set.

7. Top with cooked bacon before serving

Strawberry Pancakes

Preparation time: 15 minutes

Total time: 30 minutes

Yield: 4

Ingredients:

2 cups strawberries sliced

2 cups whole wheat flour

1 ½ tablespoons maple syrup

2 and ½ teaspoons baking powder

⅛ teaspoon kosher salt

2 tablespoons brown sugar

½ teaspoon cinnamon

2 eggs

1 and ½ cups milk

2 tablespoons clarified butter

½ teaspoon vanilla extract

Directions:

1. In a bowl, combine strawberries and syrup. Set aside 1 hour.

2. In another bowl, combine flour with baking powder, brown sugar, cinnamon and salt.

3. In a third bowl, whisk together eggs and milk.

4. Add flour mixture to eggs and stir again.

5. Add melted butter and vanilla extract and stir.

6. Heat skillet to medium and pour ¼ cup of batter in it. Cook for 2 minutes or until bubbles appear. Then flip over and brown it on the other side.

7. Repeat until all batter is used. Serve pancakes with strawberries on top.

Desserts

Balsamic Berries

Preparation time: 5 minutes

Total time: 15 minutes

Yield: 4

Ingredients:

1 cup balsamic vinegar

3 ½ cups fresh mixed berries

½ cup sliced almonds (optional)

Directions:

1. Pour balsamic vinegar into medium size saucepan and heat to medium high.

2. Allow vinegar to begin boiling then reduce heat to low and simmer 10 minutes, stirring often.

3. Once the vinegar forms a syrupy consistency, remove from heat and cool to room temperature.

4. Combine berries and almonds in a bowl and drizzle with balsamic vinegar reduction.

5. To save remaining balsamic reduction, store in an air tight container and refrigerate.

Nutty Baked Apples

Preparation time: 10 minutes

Total time: 30 minutes

Yield: 4

Ingredients:

4 apples

¼ cup raisins

¼ cup walnuts chopped

1 tablespoon cinnamon

1 tablespoon honey

Directions:

1. Preheat oven to 375 degrees F.

2. Core apples, fill each with raisins and walnuts, sprinkle cinnamon on them and drizzle honey.

3. Arrange in a glass baking dish and bake for 20 minutes.

4. Remove apples and allow to cool down for 5 minutes. Then serve.

Pumpkin Cookies

Preparation time: 15 minutes

Total time: 30 minutes

Yield: 24

Ingredients:

2 and ½ cups almond flour

¼ teaspoon salt

½ teaspoon baking soda

1 tablespoon ground flax seeds

3 tablespoons water

½ cup mashed pumpkin flesh

¼ cup honey

2 tablespoons coconut butter

1 teaspoon vanilla extract

½ cup chocolate chips

Directions:

1. Preheat oven to 350 degrees F.

2. In a mixing bowl, combine flax seeds and water. Set aside.

3. In another bowl, combine flour, salt and baking soda.

4. In a third bowl, combine honey, pumpkin, butter, and vanilla extract.

5. Pour flax seed mixture into pumpkin mixture and stir until combined.

6. Pour flour mixture into pumpkin mixture stirring throughout.

7. Fold in chocolate chocolate chips.

8. Scoop 1 tablespoon of cookie dough on a baking dish lined with parchment paper and flatten with your fingers.

9. Repeat this with the rest of the cookies. Then bake for 12-15 minutes.

10. Remove cookies from the oven, allow to cool down and serve.

Blueberry Lemon Curd

Preparation time: 10 minutes

Total time: 20 minutes

Yield: 3

Ingredients:

2 cups blueberries

¼ cup lemon juice

⅔ cup agave nectar

4 cups water

2 teaspoons lemon zest

4 tablespoons clarified butter softened

3 egg yolks

Directions:

1. Heat a small saucepan to medium and add blueberries and lemon juice.

2. Stir, bring to a simmer and cook until blueberries are soft.

3. Pour through a strainer and mash lightly into a double boiler bowl.

4. Add water to the boiler, bring to a boil, reduce heat and simmer.

5. Add nectar and butter to blueberries and blend well.

6. Whisk eggs and add to blueberry mixture.

7. Stir constantly and keep temperature at 175 degrees F until it thickens.

8. Pour in small jars and leave to cool down completely. Then serve.

Rhubarb Pie

Preparation time: 15 minutes

Total time: 65 minutes

Yield: 8

Ingredients:

1 and ½ cups almond flour

⅛ teaspoon salt

8 tablespoons cold clarified butter cut in pieces

1 teaspoon brown sugar

5 tablespoons ice water

For the filling:

3 cups rhubarb chopped

1 and ½ cups honey

3 tablespoons almond flour

½ teaspoon nutmeg

2 eggs

1 tablespoon clarified butter

⅛ teaspoon salt

2 tablespoons almond milk

Directions:

1. Preheat oven to 400 degrees F.

2. In a mixing bowl, combine 1 and ½ cups flour, salt

and sugar.

3. Add 8 tablespoons of butter and work the dough with your fingers.

4. Add ice water and mix again.

5. Transfer dough to a floured working surface, knead it, shape a fattened disk, wrap in plastic and keep in the fridge for 30 minutes.

6. Remove dough, roll a circle, arrange in a pie plate and set aside.

7. In a bowl, combine rhubarb with a pinch of salt, honey, 3 tablespoons flour and nutmeg.

8. In another bowl, mix eggs with milk and whisk well.

9. Pour dry ingredients into wet ingredients and stir well.

10. Pour the rhubarb mix in pie shell and bake for 55 minutes.

11. Remove from oven and let pie cool completely before cutting and serving.

Brown Sugar Cherry Cobbler

Preparation time: 1 hour

Total time: 2 hours

Yield: 12

Ingredients:

1 cup almond flour

1 cup brown sugar

½ cup clarified butter

1 teaspoon baking powder

2 cups sour cherries pitted

¾ cup maple syrup

1 cup milk

1 tablespoon almond flour

1 tablespoon brown sugar

2 tablespoons maple syrup

Directions:

1. Preheat oven to 350 degrees F.

2. Place butter in a baking dish allow it to melt in the oven for about 5 minutes. Then remove from the oven and set aside.

3. In a bowl, combine 1 cup flour with 1 cup sugar, baking powder and 1 cup milk.

4. Pour this mix over melted butter. Do not stir.

5. Place cherries, 1 tablespoon flour and sugar in a bowl. Toss to coat.

6. Place cherries evenly over the batter from baking dish. Do not stir.

7. Drizzle syrup over cherries and bake for 60 minutes.

8. Remove from oven, allow cobbler to cool, cut and serve.

Drinks

Melon Delight

Preparation time: 15 minutes

Total time: 15 minutes

Yield: 2

Ingredients:

2 ripe melons cubed

Equal parts lime juice and pure maple syrup

Ice for serving

Directions:

1. Place melon cubes in a pitcher, add lime juice and maple syrup.

2. Cover and keep in the fridge until you serve.

3. Pour in tall glasses and serve with ice.

Cucumber Limeade

Preparation time: 10 minutes

Total time: 10 minutes

Yield: 4

Ingredients:

1 cup cucumbers, peeled and chopped

1 and ½ cups water

1 cup lime juice

Ice

Cucumber slices for serving

For the ginger and lime syrup:

1 cup honey

1 cup ginger finely chopped

2 cups water

1 and ½ tablespoons lime zest

Directions:

1. Add water to a medium saucepan and heat to medium. Add honey, ginger and lime zest and cook about 7 minutes stirring constantly.

2. Remove mixture from heat and pour through a strainer.

3. Meanwhile, put cucumbers and 1 and ½ cups water in a blender and puree.

4. Transfer to a pitcher, add lime juice, syrup and ice and stir gently.

5. Garnish with cucumber slices and serve.

Ginger Mint Lemonade

Preparation time: 5 minutes

Total time: 35 minutes

Yield: 4

Ingredients:

½ cup mint leaves chopped

⅓ cup ginger grated

⅓ cup honey

2 cups boiling water

2 lemons juiced and strained

1 and ½ cups cold water

Ice cubes for serving

Fresh mint leaves for serving

Directions:

1. In a blender, combine hot water, mint, honey and ginger. Let sit for 20 minutes.

2. Add lemon juice and cold water. Blend until well mixed.

3. Pour in a tall glass, add ice cubes and garnish with fresh mint leaves.

PB&J Smoothie

Preparation time: 5 minutes

Total time: 5 minutes

Yield: 1

Ingredients:

¾ cup blueberries

1 cup baby kale

2 tablespoons natural peanut butter, strained

¾ cup almond milk

¼ cup plain yogurt

½ cup strawberries

½ cup ice

Directions:

1. Place berries and yogurt in blender and pulse a few times.

2. Add kale and blend again.

3. Add milk and pulse a few more times.

4. Add peanut butter, and pulse until well combined. Pour in a glass and serve.

Strawberry Avocado Summer Smoothie

Preparation time: 6 minutes

Total time: 6 minutes

Yield: 2

Ingredients:

½ frozen banana

2 cups frozen strawberries cut in halves

3 tablespoons spearmint

1 and ½ cups coconut water

½ avocado

Directions:

1. Place bananas and strawberries in blender and pulse a few times.

2. Add coconut water and avocado and blend again.

3. Add spearmint but reserve some for garnish.

4. Pour in a glass and garnish with spearmint.

Lean Green Smoothie

Preparation time: 5 minutes

Total time: 5 minutes

Yield: 2

Ingredients:

1 ripe banana

1 peeled apple

1 cup kale

1 cup spinach

1 tablespoon chia seed

¾ cup orange juice

½ cup almond milk

1 cup ice cubes

Directions:

1. Place ice, chia seeds, orange juice, banana and apple in blender and pulse.

2. Add kale, spinach, and milk. Blend until combined.

3. Pour in a glass and serve.

About the Author

Colleen Seward discovered how to live a natural healthy lifestyle after struggling for years with poor health and terrible eating habits. She grew tired diet trends that didn't provide lasting results. She then began a journey to holistically change her lifestyle; heart, body, and mind. In the process, she discovered how easy it was to live a healthy lifestyle balanced with the occasional indulgence. Colleen loves living life and eating well. Writing has given her the ability to share her experience with others.

About the Publisher

MouseWorks Publishing is an indie publisher based out of Denton, TX. Founded in 2016, our mission is simple: make books you want to read!

Follow us and be the first to know about new releases and free promotions!

http://www.facebook.com/mouseworkspub

http://www.twitter.com/mouseworkspub

Made in the USA
Middletown, DE
12 May 2019